The Life and Prayers of
Saint Francis of Assisi
Wyatt North

Wyatt North Publishing

© **Wyatt North Publishing, LLC 2012**
A Boutique Publishing Company

D0754030

About Wyatt North Publishing

Wyatt North Publishing is a boutique publishing company. We always provide high quality, perfectly formatted, Books.

We guarantee our Books. If you are not 100% satisfied we will do everything in our power to make you happy. Visit WyattNorth.com for more information. Please feel free to contact us with any questions or comments. We welcome your feedback by email at info@WyattNorth.com.

Foreword

Introducing an exciting new series from Wyatt North Publishing. **The Life and Prayers** series combines professionally researched and written biographies of iconic Christian figures with an anthology of prayers.

The Life and Prayers of Saint Francis of Assisi is the second book in this wonderful series. One part biography, one part prayer book, Saint Francis of Assisi is an essential book for any Christian.

Saint Francis of Assisi is quite possibly the most popular of all Christian saints. Perhaps it is his adoration for all living things or his unrelenting generosity that has made so many people open their hearts to him. Perhaps it is the deep conviction and piety expressed not only by the saint himself, but in his name, in the Franciscan orders throughout the centuries.

Whatever the reason, in a world that is quickly developing in a direction diametrically opposite to the saint's own simple asceticism, Saint Francis of Assisi still stirs strong emotions and compassion. How close he found God, in the very nature around him, is inspiring.

The Life of Saint Francis

I. Introduction

Saint Francis of Assisi is quite possibly the most popular of all Christian saints. Perhaps it is his adoration for all living things or his unrelenting generosity that has made so many people open their hearts to him. Perhaps it is the deep conviction and piety expressed not only by the saint himself, but in his name, in the Franciscan orders throughout the centuries.

Whatever the reason, in a world that is quickly developing in a direction diametrically opposite to the saint's own simple asceticism, Saint Francis of Assisi still stirs strong emotions and compassion. How close he found God, in the very nature around him, is inspiring.

But we are also taken by how unlikely Saint Francis' story is. Not in the respect that it rings untrue; it is easy to unearth how Francis' path developed. Rather, it is surprising. The young man we first get to know, a strutting boisterous peacock, feathered in abundant wealth, is so unlike the unassuming and impoverished ascetic. Even so we see gentleness, generosity, and a deep emotional sensitivity that is consistent throughout the saint's life.

The man we are about to meet was, in the prime of his life, a short and exceedingly slight man. He had very fair skin, yet his eyes and his hair were dark. His features were small and angular. Later in life he wore his hair in the tonsure style, the top of his head shaved and his remaining dark hair growing in a crown around his head. From the earliest days of his order, he wore a dark tunic or robe, tied shut with a simple cord, and no sandals.

He was incredibly charismatic, although later sources have called him physically unattractive.

He certainly did not start out as a man of letters, but Saint Francis did write for himself and left us texts in his own words to learn about his life and his spiritual thoughts. Aside from the rules he wrote for his order, several letters remain, as do prayers and the Testament of Saint Francis. Aside from Saint Francis' own writings, numerous people, contemporaries and successors alike have written down the life of the saint. The earliest biography was commission by Pope Gregory IX and written by a Thomas of Celano in 1230, just four years after Saint Francis' death. Other notable early writings on the life of Saint Francis include the works of Saint Bonaventure and the collection known as Fioretti di San Francesco (*The Little Flowers of Saint Francis*), which contains important clues about how the life and works of Saint Francis were seen outside of the Franciscan Order

II. The Early Years

Saint Francis was born into a time when the Christian world was effectively split into two parts. The church had divided 127 years earlier into one eastern church, which became the Eastern Orthodox Church, and one western church, which is now the Roman Catholic Church. Enmity was clearly established. In fact, only one month after Saint Francis' baptism there was a great massacre in Constantinople, known now as the Massacre of the Latins. It was a gruesome event, in which eastern Christians slaughtered western Christians, men, women and children alike.

But, it was not just the Christian world that was divided into two when Francis was born. It was also the Italy that he was born into. Not yet a unified country, it consisted of various small communities, usually under the leadership of either the Pope or the Holy Roman Emperor. Assisi, the birth-town of Saint Francis, was an independent community. As such, it was under military pressure from other nearby communities, both those that were under the Papacy and those that were under the Holy Roman Empire.

Even Assisi itself was split into two opposing fractions: the *boni homines* and the *popolo*. In essence, the boni homines were rural landholders and the popolo were urban merchants. These political fractions tore at the fiber of the community with great clashes about matters such as real estate and taxation.

Saint Francis was born into a popolo family. His father, Pietro di Bernardone, was a cloth merchant, although his origins were probably more humble than that. His entry into the textile business came through his French wife Pica. The business, or at least the foundation for the business, came to Pietro as part of his wife's dowry. He was probably trained in part by his father-in-law. Pietro and Pica owned their own house in Assisi, a valuable piece of real estate on the Via San Paolo, right next to the busy commercial district. They were by no means an aristocratic family, but they had considerable wealth.

Francis was born either in 1181 or in 1182. He had at least one brother, whose name was Angelo. It is uncertain whether Angelo was an older brother or a younger one, but as he was often known as "the son of Pica" rather than "the son of Pietro," historians believe that he was an older half-brother of Francis.

Francis would have been baptized on March 28, 1182. It was the custom in Italy at the time to baptize all healthy newborns at the city font at the cathedral of San Rufino during the Easter Vigil on Holy Sunday. Pica went alone, for Pietro was away on business in France. The baby boy was given the Christian name Giovanni. When Pietro returned, however, he never called the boy by his Christian name. Instead he called the child *Francesco*, meaning "Frenchy," because he had a certain love for all things French. So goes the legend of how Francis got his name. It should be noted that while the name did not gain popularity until after Saint Francis' time, naming a child Francesco was not unheard of for the time period.

The earliest biographers say very little about Francis' childhood, but judging from the statue of his family and the time and place that he was born into it is likely that he was sent to school at the hospital of San Giorgio in order to be educated to follow in his father's footsteps. At school, he would have learned basic Latin, enough to write some not very grammatical rudimentary prose. It is also apparent from his later life that he learned enough French to have a conversation and to sing popular French songs. When he was old enough, around 1195, he would have joined his father in the business as an apprentice and it is possible that his father took him to France on business trips, where Francis would have been able to polish his French a bit.

As a teenager Francis was extremely extroverted. Some have

said that he was in fact vain and narcissistic. He wore fine silk and woolen clothes, as was befitting a man of his means, but he added to them worn and mismatching patches to achieve a clownish effect. He constantly violated conventions and acted completely contrary to what was expected of him. He was the leader of a *societas iuvenum*, a boy's club typical of 12th century Italian cities, which he liked to engage in loud and boisterous parties and through numerous pranks. With these rich friends of his, he lead a life of leisure and was famously cavalier about expenses. Francis was also very taken with all things aesthetically pleasing, to the point where he shunned all things ugly. Lepers in particular made him wretch. When they came his way on the street, he would hold his nose and run the other way.

Francis might have wanted to be the center of attention, but he was not a malicious boy. The pranks of the societas were not terribly malign and there is no evidence that he was given to fighting or lechery. Evidence suggests that Francis was often a well-mannered young man, and sensitive. Historians note that he was particularly polite to women.

When he was 19 years old, Francis served in the communal militia. It took him into battle against the city of Perugia in 1202, which wanted to claim Assisi for the Papacy. Because Francis was rich enough to afford a horse he served with the mounted troops.

It was not a good time to be on the side of Assisi. After seeing a great many of his comrades die in the field, Francis was made a prisoner of war. Because he had his own horse, he was assumed by the Perugians to be of the knightly aristocracy and was therefore imprisoned under better conditions than many others. Even so, being a prisoner of war for over a year is not a pleasant experience. Though it is said that Francis behaved admirably in prison, reconciling arguing prisoners and befriending those shunned by others, the fact also remains that when he was released, probably in late 1203, Francis' health had been seriously damaged. He was no longer himself. He was introverted. He had nightmares and flashbacks. He spent the days wandering his father's house, listless, erratic, and unsure of himself. A modern interpretation might be to say that Francis was suffering from depression and symptoms similar to those of post-traumatic stress disorder. When his friends tried to engage him in their old partying ways, Francis' response lacked the luster of his teens.

He spent more than a year in this state, until suddenly, in April 1205, it seemed like he snapped out of it. Francis had the chance to go on yet a military campaign, this time in the far south of Italy to support the claim of the Holy Roman Emperor, Frederick II, on the throne of Sicily. But Francis' heart and mind was in a far away place. To those around him, his behavior seemed irrational.

He bought a new warhorse, new armor, and new weapons. Then he gave it all away to a knight poorer than himself and had to start over. Once he had bought himself yet another horse, new armor, and new weapons, he set out for the south with a squire. But, he only got one day's journey south of Assisi, to the city of Spoleto, before he concluded that it was a bad idea to follow a vassal into war, rather than the emperor himself who would not be participating. Therefore, he gave up the idea of going to war and turned back home. Only halfway back, in a city called Foligno, he sold his arms and horse and walked the final miles.

Before he reached Assisi, only two miles south of the town, he found the church of San Damiano. Thomas of Celano wrote that "perfectly changed in heart and soon to be changed in body, Francis was strolling one day near the old church of San Damiano, which was nearly destroyed and abandoned by all. The spirit led him to enter the church and pray."

Francis lay down and prostrated himself in front of the crucifix in prayer and was then moved by powerful and unusual visions. It seemed that the Savior on the cross moved his lips and spoke to him. "Francis," the Savior said. "go and repair my house, which, as you see, is completely destroyed." Francis was so moved by the vision that he found the priest of the church, Don Peter, and asked him if he could spend the night.

III. A Crisis of Faith

In the morning, Francis walked the last two miles home. But, he was irrevocably changed by the experience at San Damiano. Francis lost interest in his father's business and stopped going to work. He withdrew even further into himself and often spent his days hiding in his bedroom.

Enlightenment era thinkers have interpreted this as a new sense of humility, given to Francis straight by God on the day when he had the vision of the speaking Savior. Regardless of how the change came about, there was certainly a spiritual element to this new twist in Francis' personal crisis. He started to perform traditional works of penance, such as alms-giving, prayer, and even bodily mortification. On the occasions that he left the house, he gave money to every beggar that asked him, and when he ran out of money he literally gave the shirt off his back. Where he had once been charitable towards his wealthy friends, he had become charitable towards impoverished strangers.

Having considered the words of the Savior in his vision, Francis came to the conclusion that the Lord wanted him to repair the churches around Assisi, many of which were in terrible disrepair, including San Damiano itself, where Francis had the vision. He began to send furnishings anonymously to some of the poorer churches. When he felt that this was not enough, he made a pilgrimage to Rome, where he ended up exchanging clothes with a beggar and begging for alms himself. When he begged, he did so in French, effectively adopting a character slightly different from the real Francis. This would be his way for the rest of his life.

Although the changes in Francis can from our point of view seem very meaningful, they were changes that deeply troubled his father Pietro. We can easily see why. His once happy and carefree son, an extrovert loved by many who took pleasure in working alongside of his father, came back from war a shell of a man with no spirit and no joy for life. He then descended into more erratic behavior, wasting all of his money, while refusing to work, often refusing to see people, and physically hurting himself. Even the most understanding parent would be concerned that madness was involved. One by one, Francis' friends had fallen away. They could not cope with his new and unusual behavior. No longer did he want to spend time with them doing the things they had always done. Instead, he wandered the woods and spent hours in solitude in the caves around the city. He also suffered demonic fears and what must have seemed to others as hallucinations. He was so terrified of what demons might do to him that once when he saw a hunchback woman in Assisi, he doubled his repetitive actions out of fear of becoming a hunchback himself.

Francis often returned to the church of San Damiano, where he had seen Jesus speak on the cross. He would sit there and pray, or simply contemplate the passions of his Savior. It would touch his sensitive soul to such a degree that he would weep uncontrollably. His strong feelings and desire to unite with Christ his Savior caused him to mortify his body even more savagely. Later biographers have noted a prayer of Saint Francis' from these early days at San Damiano. If not exact in its verbiage, at least it may convey the spirit of his prayers there.

Most high glorious God,
enlighten the darkness of my heart and give me true Faith, and perfect Charity;
give me perception and knowledge, Lord,
that I might carry out your holy and true command.

Sometime at the end of 1205, Francis left the house of his parents to pray at San Damiano and simply did not return home. During the past six months he had become increasingly moody and isolated. Now he was simply gone. He attached himself to

San Damiano as a lay brother and went into hiding from his family for a full month. When he finally dared to show himself on the streets again he was so dirty and emaciated that people in the street thought he was a starving madman, threw things at him, and called him names. This was more than Pietro could handle. He went out and collected his son and locked him up in his room, where he tried for many days to reason with him and to convince him to give up his new and corporally unhealthy ways. Francis refused to listen to him, and when Pietro went away on business Francis' mother Pica let him out. Again he fled to San Damiano.

For Pietro there was more at stake than simply his relationship with his son and his son's mental and physical health. It was also a matter of the family business and the future of the family. Because the family business was part of Pica's dowry, it would be passed to her sons, namely Angelo and Francis upon her death. Angelo was a prudent businessman and did his part for the family business, but since returning from war Francis had squandered everything he had. Should Pica die, Pietro would lose the business to Angelo and Francis, and Francis would, most likely, give everything away and utterly ruin Angelo.

Pietro made one final attempt to talk what he thought was sense into his son. He found him at San Damiano, but Francis was in such a tearful state after contemplating the passion of Christ that Pietro could not communicate with him. Francis, for his part, managed to understand that there was an issue about money, and offered his father his purse, but would not listen to the actual issue at hand. To save Angelo's inheritance, Pietro went to the city magistrates to exclude Francis from any claims to Pica's dowry, probably on account of insanity. The city sent a bailiff to summon Francis before the tribunal, but Francis considered himself an ecclesiastical person now that he was attached to the church, layman or not, and refused to come before a secular court. The case was remanded to Bishop Guido II and Francis met his father, mother and brother again in ecclesiastical court.

The bishop was not as interested in seeing one side win as he was to make them reconcile, and he urged Francis to renounce all of his claims to his mother's dowry. Francis then left the room suddenly, removed the clothes associated with his family and station, and stripped down to his penitent's hair shirt before reentering the room. He returned his old clothing to his father and told the court: "Until now I have called Pietro di Bernardone my father. But, because I have proposed to serve God, I return to him the money on account of which he was so upset, and also all the clothing which was his, wanting to say from now on: 'Our father who art in heaven' and not 'My father, Pietro di Bernardone'."

Thomas of Celano tells us, "the bishop, sensing his intention and admiring his constancy, rose and wrapped his arms around Francis, covering him with his own robe. He saw clearly that Francis was divinely inspired and that his action contained a mystery. Thus he became Francis' helper, cherishing and comforting him."

It may have been the last time that Francis spoke to members of his family.

IV. First Disciples

It would be easy for us to assume that the true converting moment of Francis' life was in that moment, when he renounced his family in favor of the Lord. Francis did not see it that way. In his own view, his true conversion came a little while later.

Some time during the end of 1206, Francis was walking through the forests around Assisi again. This time, because it was winter, they were cold and covered with ice and snow. He was praying to God when robbers overcame him. He had nothing of value, but they beat him, stripped him and left him to die there in the cold. Somehow, Francis managed to get himself to San Verecondio, a monastery in nearby Vallingegno, where he was clothed and fed. For a while after that, he lived with an acquaintance in Gubbio. It was not until he finally returned to Assisi after his robbery that he had his true moment of conversion.

When he returned to Assisi, Francis lodged in a leprosarium. It is not known which one, but there are three candidates: San Rufino dell'Arce, San Lazzaro, or San Salvatore delle Pareti. At the leprosarium, Francis earned his keep by caring for the lepers. He cleaned the poor unfortunate lepers and dressed their wounds for them. Francis who previously had held his nose and ran the other way when he saw a leper. For the first time he saw their humanity and their beauty. He felt like he had been entirely remade by God and was finally ready to live up to the words he had uttered to the bishop on that fateful day when he renounced his earthly family.

Francis continued to live with the lepers for some time, but eventually returned to San Damiano. The building itself could make him feel the consolation of Christ and he looked up to the priests there. "The Lord gave me, and gives me still, such faith in those priests," he wrote of them. "Were they to persecute me, I would still want to have recourse to them."

Following the commandment of the speaking Savior from several months earlier, Francis also began a project to refurbish San Damiano. He bought stones and supplies, and when he ran out of money to buy the supplies he begged for them. But, because begging never came naturally to Francis, he always did so in French.

It was during this time that Francis adopted the clothing of a brother of penance: a plain dark tunic. Although he was cared for by the men of the church, the outside world probably did not take well to this change. They abused him viciously, seeing in him, most likely, a rich boy playing at piety.

And so time passed for about a year, until one day, towards the end of 1207 or the beginning of 1208, a young man arrived from Assisi looking for Francis. His name was Bernard de Quintavalle and he had been touched by Francis' devotion to God. "Brother Francis," he said, "I am disposed in heart wholly to leave the world, and to obey thee in all things as thou shalt command me." And so he joined Francis as his first disciple. Around the same time came another man from Assisi to join Francis as well. His name was Peter. Together, the three of them were lay penitents loosely attached to the church of San Damiano.

Although he had lead a societas in his former life, Francis was not really a natural leader. At least not in the respect that he enjoyed leadership. Having devoted his life to God, he wanted more than anything simply to follow. Therefore he did not quite know what to do with his two new disciples, nor indeed if he was meant to have disciples. The issue bothered him. He himself expressed his frustration in the Testament he wrote during his final days: "And when God gave me brothers, no one showed me what I should do."

Luckily for Francis, God was there to tell him exactly what he needed to do, and Francis was ready to listen. Together with his two new followers he went, on April 16, 1208, to ask a local priest to perform a *sortes biblicae*, a then popular method of divining the will of God on a specific matter. The priest performing the sortes biblicae would open the Bible up to a random page and read out the verse his finger landed upon. He would do this three times. The three verses would answer the question at hand. Because entire Bibles were expensive and not commonly held even by all priests, Francis had to have his answer divined from a copy of the New Testament alone, and because neither Francis, Bernard or Peter spoke Latin, the verses had to translated and interpreted for them by the priest.

The first time the priest opened the book he landed upon these words of Jesus: "You are lacking in one thing. Go, sell what you have, and give to the poor and you will have treasure in heaven; then come, follow me." (Mark 10:21) The second commandment that the priest pointed to was: "Take nothing for the journey, neither walking stick, nor sack, nor food, nor money, and let no one take a second tunic." (Luke 9:3) On his third attempt he came upon: "If anyone wishes to come after me, he must deny himself and take up his cross daily and follow me." (Luke 9:23) Together, the four men agreed, the verses called for a fairly extreme renunciation of all worldly things. Francis, Bernard and Peter carefully committed the verses to memory and from that day onward those three verses would shape their lives. In essence, they were the core of the Franciscan form of life.

Francis did what he could to follow the instructions. For a year he meditated upon what he should do and came to the conclusion that if he was going to have followers at all he needed the church to sanction it. The thirteenth century was not a time to haphazardly start new religious groups, at least not unless one wanted to be persecuted as a heretic. Furthermore, Francis was very concerned about whether or not he was doing what was right by God. The local bishop, Guido II, who had been his often reluctant guide in many things religious, was away at the time and could not help Francis. Instead, Francis decided to take the matter straight to the top. He went to Rome to see the Pope. To show the Pope that it was not Francis' intention to lead others, he and Peter elected Bernard de Quintavalle as the group leader.

In Rome they ran into bishop Guido, who had a strongly negative reaction to their presence in the holy city. The bishop probably did not look too kindly on the group's development. People whom he thought of lay penitents, no different from any other, had suddenly drawn up life rules. What more, they had not had the help of an experienced ecclesiastical person like himself.

"Since he was a prudent and discreet man, the bishop began to question Francis about many things and tried to convince him that he should try the life of a monk or hermit," says Thomas of Celano. "Saint Francis humbly refused his advice as well as he could, not because he despised what the bishop suggested but because, impelled by a higher desire, he devoutly wished for something else." Francis' stubbornness finally won out and the bishop agreed to introduce Francis to someone who might help him: Cardinal Colonna.

The cardinal received Francis, but, feeling that the group was nothing but regular lay hermits playacting the life of monks, he advised them to leave the busy pope alone. Francis spoke to the cardinal for several days before convincing him to speak to the pope on the group's behalf. The cardinal must have thought that the group stood a chance to gain some kind of recognition from the pope, given Pope Innocent's many bold moves to reconcile heretical groups with the church, and his strong encouragement of lay evangelicalism. For this meeting, the cardinal was the legal representative of the group in an official meeting with Pope Innocent.

The cardinal sketched out the group's intentions for the pope, who must have thought them quite like all other heretical preaching groups, but a cardinal and a bishop backing its orthodoxy were good credentials. Within a few days the matter was discussed in the papal curia. In the end, the pope approved the group. Francis probably never attended these meetings, and if he did he would not have understood the Latin debate. In the end, Francis' group was invited to come up to the pope to receive his apostolic blessing. "Go with the Lord, brothers," Pope Innocent said, "and preach penance to all as the Lord will inspire you. Then, when the Lord increases you in number and in grace, return joyously to me. At that time I will concede more to you and commit greater things to you more confidently."

It was not exactly what Francis was expecting. The pope probably saw the group mostly as lay preachers, even though Francis had never truly preached before and merely tried to promote penitence by example. This new commandment would have troubled Francis. Likewise, he must have been quite concerned that the pope's words gave implicit approval of his way of life, but not explicit.

V. A Local Order

Cardinal Colonna knew that the group would be met with suspicion by the public, so he did what he could to give them a bit of official public status. He had them tonsured, the distinctive hair cut that would mark them as clerics and as orthodox Catholics. It was about all he could do for them on his own.

The night before Francis, Bernard, and Peter begun their travels back to Assisi, Francis had a dream. In his dream, he saw a big beautiful tree, and when he tried to seek shelter under it he grew so tall that he could place his hand at the top of the tree and bend it down to where he stood on the ground. The dream, Francis felt, was the proof that God had made the Church bend and that his quest was divinely guided.

Laymen preaching penance, as the group was now expected to do, was nothing new or unusual. It had been common in Italy for at least 100 years. However, many of these lay preachers had the benefit of having studied the gospels with a priest. None of the men in Francis' group had done any such thing, and Francis himself knew only very rudimentary Latin.

About two miles outside of Assisi, Francis found an abandoned old shed and the group settled there. This stay lasted for about three months, in 1209. Francis, Bernard, and Peter lived there in poverty, feeding themselves by doing manual labor for anyone willing to pay them, and begged when they could not get food from work. Francis also decided that they needed to start "carrying the cross" as God had told them when they sought out a priest for the sortes biblicae. Their interpretation of this verse at the time was rather literal. They altered regular peasant smocks to take on a T shape. This cross they wore, bound by a cord rather than a leather belt. With the smock they wore trousers, as was the habit of travelers at the time, unlike monks living in a monastery.

On April 23, 1209, a fourth man from Assisi joined their band. His name was Giles and, since the first three were now tonsured by Cardinal Colonna, he was the first true lay brother.

Francis and the brothers did very little in terms of preaching and did not actively seek to recruit members. Nonetheless, the group grew slowly but steadily.

When the group grew too big for the old shed, Francis went to Bishop Guido to ask for a church of their own in which to pray and sing. The bishop denied their request. Nor were they allowed to stay at San Damiano. The answer came from the Benedictine monks on Monte Subasio, who offered them a ruined chapel, the Santa Maria degli Angeli, in Porziuncula. To make sure that Francis and his brothers could not evoke the principle of prescription to become owners of the chapel, they had to lease it for the symbolic sum of one basket of fish per year.

At Santa Maria degli Angeli, the brothers constructed whattle-and-daub cells around the chapel to live in. Suddenly, they were a small monastic community.

Around this time, Francis would often travel around neighboring villages by foot. He was especially drawn to the many decaying houses of worship he found there. Remembering the words of his Savior on the cross, that day in San Damiano when he had his first vision, he felt compelled to do something about the state of the churches. When he came upon one that was dirty he would sweep it. He would even wash the altar linens, unasked.

Francis also gained an increasing reputation for having a special connection with animals. On his walks in the forest, he would speak to these brothers and sisters as if they were equals, and when he returned to his disciples he would give them animal names of their own. Francis could not bear the thought of any of God's creatures injured or pained, so when it rained he would pick up worms from the road to set them aside in safety so that people would not tread on them. He set free the hare someone had trapped for him to eat, threw back the fish someone had caught for him, and he traded his own cloak to rescue lambs that were to be sold as meat.

Most of all, Francis loved swallows. His earliest biographer tells us that he preached to them. "My sisters the swallows, it's my turn to speak now, because you've already said enough," he said to the chattering birds. "Listen to the word of God. Stay still and be quiet until it's over." And to the amazement of the people around him the birds immediately quieted down and did not finish until Francis had finished preaching. Everyone could then see that he was clearly a man of God and hurried to touch his clothing.

The town of Gubbio was experiencing trouble with a wolf. The magnificent beast was devouring not only the animals of the town, but the men as well. Unafraid, Francis went out to speak to "Brother Wolf" and asked the animal to stop killing. The animal promised to mend his ways, and together they walked into town. There, Francis told the townsfolk that Brother Wolf acted out of hunger, and if they would feed him then he would promise to leave them all alone. And so it was.

The slow but steady growth of Francis' group continued. They were primarily laymen, but in those early years they were joined by at least one priest: Don Silvester. Having a priest brought a new dimension to the group, as Don Silvester was trained to sing the Mass and he could teach others to sing the Office. He also brought with him the liturgical books and instruments that the group lacked. Their small monastic community could finally have proper worship.

For at least three years, they remained a quite small band of penitents. Despite their monastic appearance, they were neither an official order nor a confraternity. Everything was still very unofficial.

After three years at the Santa Maria degli Angeli, in 1212, the group had finally begun to preach in earnest. They spoke in several cities in the region. Their message, like all penance preachers of the period, urged primarily peace and reconciliation. It was a message suitable for their extremely divided and controversial times.

Preaching brought about greater exposure for the group, and, for a man with Francis' magnetism, it was only natural that stories of prophecy began to circulate and his reputation for holiness and access to God spread. In particular it was Francis' special gift for consoling the depressed that came to the forefront. In the thirteenth century, depression was ascribed to diabolical powers inhabiting the body, which made Francis' ability to relieve depression a holy power in the eyes of his brothers. Through them, the townsfolk came to view Francis in the same light.

In 1212 Francis also met a young noblewoman by the name Clare di Favarone di Offreddicio. Clare was an eighteen-year-old noblewoman from a very wealthy family, and as such her parents carefully guarded her for the day when she was to be married. But Clare had a different fate in mind. She wanted to start a woman's order with Francis and join his life of penance.

Francis and Clare had several clandestine meetings, chaperoned of course, in which they discussed what to do. The eventual result was a plan for Clare to leave the secular world the same way that Francis had done seven years earlier. On Palm Sunday 1212, Clare left the family home with her sister Pacifica. They arrived at Santa Maria degli Angeli during the night and found Francis and the community there praying for them before the candlelit altar. Francis cut Clare's hair and gave her a habit to wear, like that of the brothers but with a veil for female modesty.

Francis now had a brand new problem to deal with: what should he do with his new female disciple, and where would she live? A woman could not be expected to live in a male monastic community like the one at Santa Maria degli Angeli. Francis turned once more to the Benedictines for help. With their aid, he placed Clare among the nuns of San Paolo of Batista, two and a half miles outside of Assisi. Soon, however, Francis moved her again. This time to another monastery on the other side of Assisi: the Sant'Angelo of Panzo. Clare was joined there by her sister Agnes who also wished to join Francis' group.

The family of the sisters soon arrived with soldiers to take them both home, but Clare managed to pacify her father and soon thereafter Clare and Agnes were moved out of Sant'Angelo of Panzo and placed into a community of their own at San Damiano. It became the first convent of the female Fransican movement. Bishop Guido was their protector. Francis and Clare continued to exchange letters, but from the moment she had her own order he stepped out of the picture in terms of leadership.

The years between 1213 and 1216 are an obscure period in the life of Saint Francis as well as the history of the Franciscan order, during which very little has been written. The group must have been affected by the Fourth Lateran Council, which took place in November 1215. This council required, amongst other things, that all religious orders hold Chapters, a meeting so called because they were meant for reading Chapters from the Bible, at least annually. It is clear that such an annual meeting was in place from there on. It would also appear that during this period, the group came to be known as the Lesser Poor, differentiating them from other groups such as the Catholic Poor and the heretical Poor of Lyon.

The Lesser Poor continued to grow during this relatively quiet period and by its end, in 1216, Francis was a religious celebrity in central Italy, although his order did not yet number more than 800 people.

VI. An International Order

As Francis' reputation was growing in Italy, the Christian world was rallying for a fifth crusade. It was issued on April 1213, by Pope Innocent III, and in 1215, during the Fourth Lateran Council, a plan for recapturing Jerusalem was discussed. Already after the annual Chapter meeting in 1216, Francis sent some brothers eastward to aid the crusader movement in converting Muslims to Christianity.

During the next annual Chapter, in May 1217, Francis also selected brothers to act as ministers and lead new groups of the Lesser Poor outside of central Italy, wherever Catholicism was practiced. These first batches of ministers were sent out to northern Italy, in Lombardy and Venetia, as well as France, Germany, Hungary and Spain.

Despite their efforts, results were mixed. Within a year, many troubling dispatches arrived from the brothers abroad. Their greatest problem, it seemed, was with their lack of preparation. The brothers that Francis had sent out were not picked for credentials relating to the culture where they were going, and none of them spoke the language in the country. The sixty brothers who were sent to Germany could not explain themselves properly and were soon arrested as heretics. The envoys to Hungary found themselves abused by robbers and went back to Italy.

The men who had gone to France experienced a number of close calls, but eventually received confirmation from the new pope, Honorius III, that they were orthodox Catholics, and thus escaped being trialed as heretics. The brothers sent to Spain were lucky in that the Italian and Spanish tongues at the time were fairly similar. Their visit in Spain was largely successful for two years, until they went into Muslim North Africa and were all martyred.

Nonetheless, the word about Francis was far reaching. In 1219, an English preacher called Odo of Cheriton wrote a speech in which he mentioned Francis and it is clear from its context that the Saint needed no introduction.

Also in 1219, Francis himself decided to participate in the conversion work being carried out by the brothers. It was a desire that had been with him for several years, but the order was then not yet ready to function on its own in his absence.

Francis set his sight on Egypt. There, he asked for permission to cross into enemy territory and preach the virtues of Christ to the sultan al-Kamil. The cardinal in charge, however, saw nothing special in Francis and refused. The brothers harassed the cardinal for several days, until he relented to let them pass, on the condition that he was left out of the affair completely.

When Francis and the brothers crossed the Nile and reached the other bank they were welcomed. The Muslim soldiers must have assumed that they were deserters wanting to convert to Islam, or perhaps even envoys to discuss the surrender of the Christian forces. Francis was as linguistically unprepared to preach to the Arabs as his brothers had been to preach to the Germans, but he was cunning.

He stood his ground and he shouted repeatedly the word *soldan*, that is: sultan, until he was taken to al-Kamil. The sultan was a learned man and most likely recognized Francis as clergy, based on his tonsure. He too must have thought that peace negotiations were about to begin. When the brothers told him that they were not an embassy for the cardinal, but for Jesus Christ, however, the sultan told them plainly that he had no time for theological discussions. Also, he said, he had plenty of religious experts who could easily show them the truth of Islam.

Undeterred, Francis agreed to discuss the matter of the Messiah with the sultan's religious experts. Furthermore, he said, if he could not convince the sultan and his men to convert to Christianity he would gladly let them behead him. Impressed by Francis' zeal, the sultan allowed the debate.

The sultan's religious leaders very quickly denounced Francis as a dangerous heretic and emphatically argued for his execution. But, the sultan remained impressed and although he had no intention to convert to Christianity, he let Francis stay and had many discussions with him on religious matters. After all, the sultan had no trouble praising the virtues of Christ, himself a Muslim and therefore seeing Christ as a great prophet although no Messiah. And Francis never spoke ill of anyone, not even a man like Mohammed, whom he naturally considered a false prophet. Sultan al-Kamil offered to take care of Francis and his brothers if they converted, but the brothers refused. When it became clear that the sultan would not convert, Francis and his brothers prepared to depart. The sultan then offered them parting gifts of their choice, of gold and jewels, but they wanted only a meal for the day which merely further impressed the sultan.

Francis' feat of surviving for so long in the enemy camp also impressed the Christian clergy present at the front. The rector of the Crusader Church of Saint Michael at Acre even decided to join Francis' order, along with two other clergy

Having spent enough time in Egypt, Francis decided to follow in the footsteps of the brothers he had previously sent to the Middle East and traveled further eastwards.

VII. The Final Years

After spending a year in the Middle East, Francis went home to Italy. He had fallen quite ill, probably from Malaria, and he had received word from brothers back at the Santa Maria degli Angeli community that in his absence new rules had been made, with which Francis did not agree, and several brothers had quit the community and left to start their own groups. Never having liked being leader and making decisions for others, Francis did not know quite what to do with the new divided community he came home to find. He went to Pope Honorius III for advice. How long he had come, that he could now approach a pope on his own! Francis asked the pope to appoint for the Lesser Poor a group adviser or official leader. He had a Cardinal Hugolino in mind and the pope relented to his request. Whereas Francis did not at all like having his authority felt, Cardinal Hugolino had no such problems at all. Even so, there was never any question of where the real authority lay. Hugolino merely acted on Francis' orders.

At the end of the year, Francis suddenly resigned. His distaste for leading others had finally led him to the opposite end of the spectrum. Whereas he had always insisted that he was not above the other brothers, he now wanted to be below even the lowest of the uninitiated novices of the order. He wanted someone to always be there to tell him what to do. This change in the hierarchy terrified the brothers who often did not know how to handle it. Their former leader suddenly wanted to be reprimanded and punished, and he would often have to tell them exactly how they should go about ordering around and what punishments to dole out.

Despite having officially resigned, Francis went on to produce a new rule governing hermitages in 1221. And Francis continued to write. By spring 1223 he had produced the final document, which he considered to be his rule of life and to which he directed all of his followers. This more official way of life in the community came with yet another change: the group was increasingly being called an "order." On November 29, 1223, Francis' rule was approved by the pope, signaling to the world that the Franciscans were finally a legal established order of the Catholic Church.

Throughout Francis' retirement, the brothers had increasingly conflicted attitudes towards him. They very much wanted to revere him as a leader, but that was difficult given that he was still insisting that someone else give him commands and speak from him in all matters relating to the order. In addition to this, Francis was becoming increasingly ill and the brothers could no longer depend on him in the manner that they previously had.

Less than a month after the pope approved Francis' rule, Francis and his brothers visited the town of Greccio to celebrate Christmas. Francis so desired to understand the experience of Christ that he decided to reenact the birth of the Savior. Although nativity scenes are common today, they were completely unheard of in 1223. So as to not cause offense, he made sure that the event would be dignified and sombre. Everything had to be just right. He arranged a manger, filled it with hay and brought in oxen and asses. The brothers each had their position, holding candles and torches to reinvent the starry night sky of the Savior's birth. Jubilantly they sang, and answered each other's singing, until it was Francis' turn, as deacon, to sing the Gospel. From the manger he lift up the little doll that had been placed there to represent the infant Jesus and cradled it in his arms. And in that moment, for an instant only, eyewitnesses say, the doll was a living child.

In 1224, Francis became the first person recorded to bear the wounds of Christ's passion: the stigmata. It occurred during an intense contemplation of the Christ's passion, while Francis was performing a 40 day fast. He had prayed for an experience like that of Jesus, to feel what the Savior had felt, and it was then that a seraph came down from Heaven and imprinted Francis with the wounds of the Messiah. Francis' earliest biographer, Thomas of Celano, tells us that "his hands and feet seemed to be pierced by nails, with the heads of the nails appearing in the palms of his hands and on the upper sides of his feet, the points appearing on the other side. The marks were round on the palm of each hand but elongated on the other side, and small pieces of flesh jutting out from the rest took on the appearance of the nail-ends, bent and driven back. In the same way the marks of nails were impressed on his feet and projected beyond the rest of the flesh. Moreover, his right side had a large wound as if it had been pierced with a spear, and it often bled so that his tunic and trousers were soaked with his sacred blood."

Although Francis recovered from the stigmata, his illness continued to wreak havoc with his body. By 1225 Francis could not walk. He could barely chew and swallow his food. He was nearly blind, probably from ophthalmia, and the illness meant that light caused him pain. Eventually he had to have a piece of cloth covering his eyes to keep him in darkness, just to feel less pain. As he became worse, he also refused food and medicine. Doctors tried in vain to cure him. The flesh from his jaw to the eyebrow was cauterized by a surgeon, but Francis did not get better. He spent the winter of 1225-1226 recovering from the surgery, without truly improving. As the illness ravished his body, it was clear to all those around him that Francis was going to ascend into Heaven and continue guiding the brothers from a special place with God. His sainthood was so clear to many around him, and many who lived in the area and knew about him, that they declared it in his presence even before he drew his final breath.

It was during 1226 that Francis dictated his testament, in which he gave briefly his own version of how the order came to be, and what he desired for the brothers in the future. The doctors had told him that he would be dead before the first week of October was over and that might have been what motivated him.

The doctors, it turned out, were right. Francis died on October 3, 1226, in the community at Santa Maria degli Angeli, surrounded by those who cared about him.

VIII. A Life with Legacy

On July 16, 1228, Francis was pronounced a saint by Pope Gregory IX. His feast day is celebrated on October 4, and because of Francis' strong affiliation and the depth of his feelings for all God's creatures it is often celebrated with a blessing of animals. From time to time, a second feast day has been celebrated on September 17, in honor of the stigmata that he suffered in 1224.

Although the Franciscan Order was fraught with dissension in the years following Saint Francis' death, in particular on matters of how closely one should follow Saint Francis' testament and how much money brothers were allowed to handle, it has stood the test of time. It was already a respectable order in the final days of the saint and remains so almost 800 years later, despite the many changes in the world that has threatened its survival.

Today there are many Franciscan orders. The most prominent, and the direct descendant of Saint Francis himself, is the Order of Friars Minor, who seek to live a life closely following that monastic manner in which Francis himself lived. Since the days immediately following Saint Francis' death, Franciscans have been teaching at universities, running hospitals, and working with the urban poor. Those men are now the Order of Friars Minor Conventual. In 1520, the Order of Friars Minor Capuchin was founded as an order of very austere hermit Franciscans not allowed to so much as touch money. The eremitical ideal was eventually abandoned, but the ideal of poverty remains strong and Capuchin friars are still not allowed to manage money of their own.

The saint himself also founded the Secular Franciscan Order, which allows lay men and women to continue living within their congregations and still devote themselves to the Franciscan ideals. Also founded by the saint is, of course, the Second Order of Saint Francis, often known as the Poor Clares. These are the Franciscan nuns who have followed in the footsteps of Saint Clare, Saint Francis' first female disciple. This is to just name the most prominent. Since the Protestant Reformation in numerous countries, several Franciscan orders have been created outside of the Catholic framework. Most like the Catholic orders in their organization are perhaps the Anglican Franciscans, but there are Lutheran and non-denominational Franciscan orders as well.

Little did he know, when he was carousing in the streets of Assisi wearing his clownish patches, or when he was praying alone at San Damiano and mocked in the streets, that his life would be studied, revered, and emulated as one of the most devout and godly.

Prayers to Saint Francis

Prayer to Saint Francis of Assisi

Most lovable and popular Saint, son of a go-getting and wealthy merchant of Assisi, you discarded earthly possessions for the Savior you loved so dearly and you won innumerable persons for Jesus. How greatly we need in our day unselfish and just merchants. Inspire them with the love of Christ for others and with the desire for things that endure. Amen.

Prayer For Animals

God Our Heavenly Father, You created the world to serve humanity's needs and to lead them to You. By our own fault we have lost the beautiful relationship which we once had with all your creation. Help us to see that by restoring our relationship with You we will also restore it with all Your creation. Give us the grace to see all animals as gifts from You and to treat them with respect for they are Your creation. We pray for all animals who are suffering as a result of our neglect. May the order You originally established be once again restored to the whole world through the intercession of the Glorious Virgin Mary, the prayers of Saint Francis and the merits of Your Son, Our Lord Jesus Christ Who lives and reigns with You now and forever. Amen.

Prayer for the Feast of Saint Francis of Assisi

O God, Who, through the merits of blessed Francis, magnifies Your church, enriching it anew with spiritual offspring: make us, like him, to disdain the goods of earth, nor at any time to lack the comforting gifts of heaven.

Prayer in Honor of the Sacred Stigmata of Saint Francis of Assisi

O Lord Jesus Christ, Who when the world was growing cold, in order that the hearts of men might burn anew with the fire of Your love, did in the flesh of the most blessed Francis reproduce the stigmata of Your passion: be mindful of his merits and prayers; and in Your mercy vouchsafe to us the grace ever to carry Your cross, and to bring forth worthy fruits of penance.

To all the faithful who, upon the five Sundays which immediately precede the feast of the sacred stigmata of Saint Francis of Assisi, or upon any other five consecutive Sundays during the year, shall exercise themselves either in pious meditation, or in vocal prayer, or in any other work of Christian piety, in honor of the said sacred stigmata, a plenary indulgence is granted once a year, on each of the five Sundays, on the usual conditions.

-Pope Leo XIII, 21 November 1885

Litany in Honor of Saint Francis

Lord, have mercy on us.
Christ, have mercy on us.

Lord, have mercy on us. Christ, hear us.
Christ, graciously hear us.

God the Father of Heaven,
Have mercy on us.

God the Son, Redeemer of the world,
Have mercy on us.

God the Holy Spirit,
Have mercy on us.

Holy Trinity, One God,
Have mercy on us.

Holy Mary, conceived without sin,
Pray for us.

Holy Mary, special patroness of the three Orders of Saint Francis,
Pray for us.

Saint Francis, seraphic patriarch,
Pray for us.

Saint Francis, most prudent father,
Pray for us.

Saint Francis, despiser of the world,
Pray for us.

Saint Francis, model of penance,
Pray for us.

Saint Francis, conqueror of vices,
Pray for us.

Saint Francis, imitator of the Saviour,

Pray for us.

Saint Francis, bearer of the marks of Christ,
Pray for us.

Saint Francis, sealed with the character of Jesus,
Pray for us.

Saint Francis, example of purity,
Pray for us.

Saint Francis, image of humility,
Pray for us.

Saint Francis, abounding in grace,
Pray for us.

Saint Francis, reformer of the erring,
Pray for us.

Saint Francis, healer of the sick,
Pray for us.

Saint Francis, pillar of the Church,
Pray for us.

Saint Francis, defender of the Faith,
Pray for us.

Saint Francis, champion of Christ,
Pray for us.

Saint Francis, defender of thy children,
Pray for us.

Saint Francis, invulnerable shield,
Pray for us.

Saint Francis, confounder of the heretics,
Pray for us.

Saint Francis, converter of the pagans,
Pray for us.

Saint Francis, supporter of the lame,
Pray for us.

Saint Francis, raiser of the dead,
Pray for us.

Saint Francis, healer of the lepers,
Pray for us.

Saint Francis, our advocate,
Pray for us.

Lamb of God, Who takest away the sins of the world,
Spare us, O Lord.

Lamb of God, Who takest away the sins of the world,
Graciously hear us, O Lord.

Lamb of God, Who takest away the sins of the world,
Have mercy on us.

Christ, hear us.
Christ, graciously hear us.

V. Pray for us, O blessed father Francis,
R. That we may be made worthy of the promises of Christ.

Let Us Pray

O Lord Jesus Christ, Who,
when the world was growing cold,
in order to renew in our hearts

the flame of love,
imprinted the sacred marks of Thy Passion
on the body of our blessed father Francis,
mercifully grant that by his merits and prayers
we may persevere in bearing the cross
and may bring forth fruits worthy of penance,
Thou Who livest and reignest,
world without end.

Amen

A Prayer of Thanksgiving

All-powerful, most holy,
most high and supreme God,
Holy and just Father,
Lord King of heaven and earth,
we thank You for Yourself.
for through Your holy will
and through Your only Son
with the Holy Spirit
You have created everything spiritual and corporeal
and, after making us in Your own image and likeness,
You placed us in paradise.

Through our own fault we fell.

We thank You
for as through Your own Son You created us,
so through Your holy love
with which You loved us,
You broguht about His birth
as true God and true man
by the glorious, ever-virgin,

most blessed, holy Mary;
and You willed to redeem us captives
through His cross and blood and death.

We thank You
for Your Son Himself will come again
in the glory of His majesty
to send into the eternal fire
the wicked ones
who have not done penance
and have not known You
and to say to all those
who have known You, adored You and served You in penance:
"Come, you blessed of my Father,
receive the kingdom prepared for you
from the beginning of the world."

Because all of us, wretches and sinners,
are not worthy to pronounce Your name,
we humbly ask
our Lord Jesus Christ,
Your beloved Son,
in Whom You are well pleased,
together with the Holy Spirit,
the Paraclete,
to give You thanks,
for everything
as it pleases You and Him,
Who always satisfies You in everything,
through Whom You have done so much for us.

Alleluia!

We also thank You, most holy Father,
for all priests
who believe and teach
what Saint Francis of Assisi
expresses in this prayer,

he who had such great respect for these ordained men.
May they, because of Your grace,
always remain faithful to all the teachings
of holy Mother Church
for the spiritual benefit of Your holy People,
for the sake of Your glory.
Amen.

Alleluia.

You are Holy, Lord

You are holy, Lord,

the only God,
and Your deeds are wonderful.
You are strong.
You are great.
You are the Most High.
You are Almighty.
You, Holy Father
are King of heaven and earth.
You are Three and One,
Lord God, all Good.
You are Good,
all Good, supreme Good,
Lord God, living and true.
You are love.
You are wisdom.
You are humility.
You are endurance.
You are rest.
You are peace.
You are joy and gladness.
You are justice and moderation.

You are all our riches,
and You suffice for us.
You are beauty.
You are gentleness.
You are our protector.
You are our guardian and defender.
You are our courage.
You are our haven and our hope.
You are our faith,
our great consolation.
You are our eternal life,
Great and Wonderful Lord,
God Almighty,
Merciful Saviour.

We Adore Thee (Adarmus te)

We adore Thee,
most holy Lord Jesus Christ,
here and in all Thy churches
that are in the whole world,
and we bless Thee;
because by Thy Holy Cross
Thou hast redeemed the World.

Amen.

(IN LATIN)

Adoramus te,
sanctissime Domine Iesu Christe,
hic et ad omnes Ecclesias tuas,

quae sunt in toto mundo,
et benedicimus tibi;
quia per sanctam Crucem tuam redemisti mundum.

Amen.

Marion Prayer of Saint Francis

Salutation to the Blessed Virgin Mary

Hail, holy Lady, most holy Queen,
Mary, Mother of God, ever-virgin;
Chosen by the most holy Father in Heaven,
consecrated by Him
with His most holy and beloved Son
and the Holy Spirit, the Comforter.
On you descended
and in you still remains
all the fullness of grace and every good.
Hail, His palace.
Hail, His tabernacle.
Hail, His robe.
Hail, His handmaid.
Hail, His mother.
And hail, all holy virtues,
who by the grace
and inspiration of the Holy Spirit
are poured into the hearts
of the faithful so that,
faithless no longer,
they may be faithful servants of God through you.

Amen.

Prayers by Saint Francis

Canticle of Brother Sun

Most high, all powerful, all good Lord!
All praise is yours, all glory, all honor, and all blessing.
To you, alone, Most High, do they belong.
No mortal lips are worthy to pronounce your name.
Be praised, my Lord, through all your creatures,
especially through my lord Brother Sun,
who brings the day; and you give light through him.
And he is beautiful and radiant in all his splendor!
Of you, Most High, he bears the likeness.
Be praised, my Lord, through Sister Moon and the stars;
in the heavens you have made them bright, precious and
beautiful.
Be praised, my Lord, through Brothers Wind and Air,
and clouds and storms, and all the weather,
through which you give your creatures sustenance.
Be praised, My Lord, through Sister Water;
she is very useful, and humble, and precious, and pure.
Be praised, my Lord, through Brother Fire,
through whom you brighten the night.
He is beautiful and cheerful, and powerful and strong.
Be praised, my Lord, through our sister Mother Earth,
who feeds us and rules us,
and produces various fruits with colored flowers and herbs.
Be praised, my Lord, through those who forgive for love of you;
through those who endure sickness and trial.
Happy those who endure in peace,
for by you, Most High, they will be crowned.
Be praised, my Lord, through our Sister Bodily Death,
from whose embrace no living person can escape.

Woe to those who die in mortal sin!
Happy those she finds doing your most holy will.
The second death can do no harm to them.
Praise and bless my Lord, and give thanks,
and serve him with great humility.
Amen.

Immaculate Conception Novena Prayer

Hail, holy Lady,

Most holy Queen,
Mary, Mother of God,
Virgin made Church;
Chosen by the most holy Father in heaven,
consecrated by him,
with his most holy beloved Son
and the Holy Spirit, the Comforter.
On you descended and in you still remains
all the fulness of grace
and every good.
Hail, his Palace.
his Tabernacle.
Hail, his Robe.
Hail, his Handmaid.
Hail, his Mother.
And Hail, all holy Virtues
who, by the grace
and inspiration of the Holy Spirit,
are poured forth into the hearts of the
faithful
so that, faithless no longer,
they may be made faithful servants of God
through you.
Amen.

Instrument of Your Peace

Lord, make me an instrument of your peace.

Where there is hatred, let me sow love;
where there is injury, pardon;
where there is doubt, faith;
where there is despair, hope;
where there is darkness, light;
and where there is sadness, joy.

O Divine Master, grant that I may not so much seek
to be consoled as to console;
to be understood as to understand;
to be loved as to love.
For it is in giving that we receive;
it is in pardoning that we are pardoned;
and it is in dying that we are born to eternal life.
Amen.

Praised Be

Praised be my Lord and God, with all His creatures, and
especially our brother the sun, who brings us the day and brings
us the light; fair is he, and he shines with great splendor.

O Lord, he is a sign to us of you!

Praised be my Lord for our sister the moon, and for this stars, set
clear and lovely in the heaven.
Amen.

Stations of the Cross

The Sign of the Cross

In the name of the Father, and of the Son, and of the Holy Spirit. Amen.

Act of Contrition

O most merciful Jesus, with a contrite heart and penitent spirit, I bow down in profound humility before Your divine majesty. I adore You as my supreme Lord and Master; I believe in You, I hope in You, I love You above all things. I am heartily sorry for having offended You, my Supreme and Only Good. I resolve to amend my life, and although I am unworthy to obtain mercy, yet the sight of Your holy cross, on which You died, inspires me with hope and consolation. I will meditate on Your sufferings, and visit the stations of Your Passion in company with Your sorrowful Mother and my guardian angel, with the intention of promoting Your honor and saving my soul.

I desire to gain all the indulgences granted for this holy exercise for myself and for the Poor Souls in Purgatory. O merciful Redeemer, who has said, "And I, if I be lifted from earth, will draw all things to Myself," draw my heart and my love to You, that I may perform this devotion as perfectly as possible, and that I may live and die in union with You. Amen.

The First Station

Jesus Is Condemned to Death

We adore You, O Christ, and we praise You, because by Your holy cross, You have redeemed the world.

Jesus, most innocent, who neither did nor could commit a sin, was condemned to death, and moreover, to the most ignominious death of the cross. To remain a friend of Caesar, Pilate delivered Him into the hands of His enemies. A fearful crime – to condemn Innocence to death, and to offend God in order not to displease men!

O innocent Jesus, having sinned, I am guilty of eternal death, but You willingly accept the unjust sentence of death, that I might live. For whom, then, shall I live, if not for You, my Lord? Should I desire to please men, I could not be Your servant. Let me, therefore, rather displease men and all the world, than not please You, O Jesus.

Our Father who art in heaven, hallowed be Thy name. Thy kingdom come, Thy will be done on earth as it is in heaven. Give us this day our daily bread, and forgive us our debts as we forgive our debtors. Lead us not into temptation but deliver us from evil. Amen.

Hail Mary, full of grace. The Lord is with you. Blessed are you among women, and blessed is the fruit of thy womb. Holy Mary, Mother of God, pray for us sinners now and at the hour of our death. Amen.

Glory be to the Father, and to the Son, and to the Holy Spirit. As it was in the beginning, is now, and ever shall be, world without end. Amen.

Lord Jesus, crucified, have mercy on us!

The Second Station

Jesus is made to carry His Cross

We adore You, O Christ, and we praise You, because by Your holy cross, You have redeemed the world.

When our divine Savior beheld the cross, He willingly stretched out His bleeding arms, lovingly embraced it, tenderly kissed it, placed it on His bruised shoulders, and, though nearly exhausted, He joyfully carried it.

O my Jesus, I cannot be Your friend and follower if I refuse to carry the cross. Dearly beloved cross! I embrace You, I kiss You, I joyfully accept You from the hands of my God. Far be it from me to glory in anything save in the cross of my Lord and Redeemer. By it the world shall be crucified to me and I to the world, that I may be Yours forever.

Our Father who art in heaven, hallowed be Thy name. Thy kingdom come, Thy will be done on earth as it is in heaven. Give us this day our daily bread, and forgive us our debts as we forgive our debtors. Lead us not into temptation but deliver us from evil. Amen.

Hail Mary, full of grace. The Lord is with you. Blessed are you among women, and blessed is the fruit of thy womb. Holy Mary, Mother of God, pray for us sinners now and at the hour of our death. Amen.

Glory be to the Father, and to the Son, and to the Holy Spirit. As it was in the beginning, is now, and ever shall be, world without end. Amen.

Lord Jesus, crucified, have mercy on us!

The Third Station

Jesus falls the First Time

We adore You, O Christ, and we praise You, because by Your holy cross, You have redeemed the world.

Our dear Savior, carrying the cross, was so weakened by its weight that he fell exhausted to the ground. Our sins and misdeeds were the heavy burden which oppressed Him: the cross was to Him light and sweet, but our sins were galling and insupportable.

O my Jesus, You bore my burden and the heavy weight of my sins. Should I, then, not bear in union with You, my easy burden of suffering and accept the sweet yoke of Your commandments? Your yoke is sweet and Your burden is light: I willingly accept it. I will take up my cross and follow You.

Our Father who art in heaven, hallowed be Thy name. Thy kingdom come, Thy will be done on earth as it is in heaven. Give us this day our daily bread, and forgive us our debts as we forgive our debtors. Lead us not into temptation but deliver us from evil. Amen.

Hail Mary, full of grace. The Lord is with you. Blessed are you among women, and blessed is the fruit of thy womb. Holy Mary, Mother of God, pray for us sinners now and at the hour of our death. Amen.

Glory be to the Father, and to the Son, and to the Holy Spirit. As it was in the beginning, is now, and ever shall be, world without end. Amen.

Lord Jesus, crucified, have mercy on us!

The Fourth Station

Jesus meets His Sorrowful Mother

We adore You, O Christ, and we praise You, because by Your holy cross, You have redeemed the world.

How painful and how sad it must have been for Mary, the sorrowful Mother, to behold her beloved Son, laden with the burden of the cross! What unspeakable pangs her most tender heart experienced! How earnestly did she desire to die in place of Jesus, or at least with Him! Implore this sorrowful Mother that she assist you in the hour of your death.

O Jesus, O Mary, I am the cause of the great and manifold pains which pierce your loving hearts! Oh, that also my heart would feel and experience at least some of your sufferings! O Mother of Sorrows, let me participate in the sufferings which You and Your Son endured for me, and let me experience Your sorrow, that afflicted with You, I may enjoy Your assistance in the hour of my death.

Our Father who art in heaven, hallowed be Thy name. Thy kingdom come, Thy will be done on earth as it is in heaven. Give us this day our daily bread, and forgive us our debts as we forgive our debtors. Lead us not into temptation but deliver us from evil. Amen.

Hail Mary, full of grace. The Lord is with you. Blessed are you among women, and blessed is the fruit of thy womb. Holy Mary, Mother of God, pray for us sinners now and at the hour of our death. Amen.

Glory be to the Father, and to the Son, and to the Holy Spirit. As it was in the beginning, is now, and ever shall be, world without end. Amen.

Lord Jesus, crucified, have mercy on us!

The Fifth Station

Simon of Cyrene helps Jesus to carry His Cross

We adore You, O Christ, and we praise You, because by Your holy cross, You have redeemed the world.

Simon of Cyrene was compelled to help Jesus carry His cross, and Jesus accepted his assistance. How willingly would He also permit you to carry the cross: He calls, but you hear Him not; He invites you, but you decline. What a reproach, to bear the cross reluctantly!

O Jesus! Whosoever does not take up his cross and follow You, is not worYour of You. Behold, I join You in the Way of Your Cross; I will be Your assistant, following Your bloody footsteps, that I may come to You in eternal life.

Our Father who art in heaven, hallowed be Thy name. Thy kingdom come, Thy will be done on earth as it is in heaven. Give us this day our daily bread, and forgive us our debts as we forgive our debtors. Lead us not into temptation but deliver us from evil. Amen.

Hail Mary, full of grace. The Lord is with you. Blessed are you among women, and blessed is the fruit of thy womb. Holy Mary, Mother of God, pray for us sinners now and at the hour of our death. Amen.

Glory be to the Father, and to the Son, and to the Holy Spirit. As it was in the beginning, is now, and ever shall be, world without end. Amen.

Lord Jesus, crucified, have mercy on us!

The Sixth Station

Veronica wipes the Face of Jesus

We adore You, O Christ, and we praise You, because by Your holy cross, You have redeemed the world.

Veronica, impelled by devotion and compassion, presents her veil to Jesus to wipe His disfigured face. And Jesus imprints on it His holy countenance: a great recompense for so small a service. What return to you make to your Savior for His great and manifold benefits?

Most merciful Jesus! What return shall I make for all the benefits You have bestowed upon me? Behold I consecrate myself entirely to Your service. I offer and consecrate to You my heart: imprint on it Your sacred image, never again to be effaced by sin.

Our Father who art in heaven, hallowed be Thy name. Thy kingdom come, Thy will be done on earth as it is in heaven. Give us this day our daily bread, and forgive us our debts as we forgive our debtors. Lead us not into temptation but deliver us from evil. Amen.

Hail Mary, full of grace. The Lord is with you. Blessed are you among women, and blessed is the fruit of thy womb. Holy Mary, Mother of God, pray for us sinners now and at the hour of our death. Amen.

Glory be to the Father, and to the Son, and to the Holy Spirit. As it was in the beginning, is now, and ever shall be, world without end. Amen.

Lord Jesus, crucified, have mercy on us!

The Seventh Station

Jesus falls the Second Time

We adore You, O Christ, and we praise You, because by Your holy cross, You have redeemed the world.

The suffering Jesus, under the weight of His cross, again falls to the ground; but the cruel executioners do not permit Him to rest a moment. Pushing and striking Him, they urge Him onward. It is the frequent repetition of our sins which oppress Jesus. Witnessing this, how can I continue to sin?

O Jesus, Son of David, have mercy on me! Offer me Your helping hand, and aid me, that I may not fall again into my former sins. From this very moment, I will earnestly strive to reform: nevermore will I sin! Thou, O sole support of the weak, by Your grace, without which I can do nothing, strengthen me to carry out faithfully this my resolution.

Our Father who art in heaven, hallowed be Thy name. Thy kingdom come, Thy will be done on earth as it is in heaven. Give us this day our daily bread, and forgive us our debts as we forgive our debtors. Lead us not into temptation but deliver us from evil. Amen.

Hail Mary, full of grace. The Lord is with you. Blessed are you among women, and blessed is the fruit of thy womb. Holy Mary, Mother of God, pray for us sinners now and at the hour of our death. Amen.

Glory be to the Father, and to the Son, and to the Holy Spirit. As it was in the beginning, is now, and ever shall be, world without end. Amen.

Lord Jesus, crucified, have mercy on us!

The Eighth Station

The women of Jerusalem weep over Jesus

We adore You, O Christ, and we praise You, because by Your holy cross, You have redeemed the world.

These devoted women, moved by compassion, weep over the suffering Savior. But He turns to them, saying: "Weep not for Me, Who am innocent, but weep for yourselves and for your children." Weep You also, for there is nothing more pleasing to Our Lord and nothing more profitable for Yourself, than tears shed from contrition for Your sins.

O Jesus, Who shall give to my eyes a torrent of tears, that day and night I may weep for my sins? I beseech You, through Your bitter and bloody tears, to move my heart by Your divine grace, so that from my eyes tears may flow abundantly, and that I may weep all my days over Your sufferings, and still more over their cause, my sins.

Our Father who art in heaven, hallowed be Thy name. Thy kingdom come, Thy will be done on earth as it is in heaven. Give us this day our daily bread, and forgive us our debts as we forgive our debtors. Lead us not into temptation but deliver us from evil. Amen.

Hail Mary, full of grace. The Lord is with you. Blessed are you among women, and blessed is the fruit of thy womb. Holy Mary,

Mother of God, pray for us sinners now and at the hour of our death. Amen.

Glory be to the Father, and to the Son, and to the Holy Spirit. As it was in the beginning, is now, and ever shall be, world without end. Amen.

Lord Jesus, crucified, have mercy on us!

The Ninth Station

Jesus falls the Third Time

We adore You, O Christ, and we praise You, because by Your holy cross, You have redeemed the world.

Jesus, arriving exhausted at the foot of Calvary, falls for the third time to the ground. His love for us, however, is not diminished, not extinguished. What a fearfully oppressive burden our sins must be to cause Jesus to fall so often! Had He, however, not taken them upon Himself, they would have plunged us into the abyss of Hell.

Most merciful Jesus, I return You infinite tanks for not permitting me to continue in sin and to fall, as I have so often deserved, into the depths of Hell. Enkindle in me an earnest desire of amendment; let me never again relapse, but vouchsafe me the grace to persevere in penance to the end of my life.

Our Father who art in heaven, hallowed be Thy name. Thy kingdom come, Thy will be done on earth as it is in heaven. Give us this day our daily bread, and forgive us our debts as we forgive our debtors. Lead us not into temptation but deliver us from evil. Amen.

Hail Mary, full of grace. The Lord is with you. Blessed are you among women, and blessed is the fruit of thy womb. Holy Mary, Mother of God, pray for us sinners now and at the hour of our death. Amen.

Glory be to the Father, and to the Son, and to the Holy Spirit. As it was in the beginning, is now, and ever shall be, world without end. Amen.

Lord Jesus, crucified, have mercy on us!

The Tenth Station

Jesus is stripped of His Garments

We adore You, O Christ, and we praise You, because by Your holy cross, You have redeemed the world.

When Our Savior had arrived on Calvary, He was cruelly despoiled of His garments. How painful this must have been because they adhered to His wounded and torn body, and with them parts of His bloody skin were removed! All the wounds of Jesus were renewed. Jesus was despoiled of His garments that He might die possessed of nothing; how happy will I also die after laying aside my former self with all evil desires and sinful inclinations!

Induce me, O Jesus, to lay aside my former self and to be renewed according to Your will and desire. I will not spare myself, however painful this should be for me: despoiled of things temporal, of my own will, I desire to die, in order to live for You forever.

Our Father who art in heaven, hallowed be Thy name. Thy kingdom come, Thy will be done on earth as it is in heaven. Give us this day our daily bread, and forgive us our debts as we forgive our debtors. Lead us not into temptation but deliver us from evil. Amen.

Hail Mary, full of grace. The Lord is with you. Blessed are you among women, and blessed is the fruit of thy womb. Holy Mary, Mother of God, pray for us sinners now and at the hour of our death. Amen.

Glory be to the Father, and to the Son, and to the Holy Spirit. As it was in the beginning, is now, and ever shall be, world without end. Amen.

Lord Jesus, crucified, have mercy on us!

The Eleventh Station

Jesus is nailed to the Cross

We adore You, O Christ, and we praise You, because by Your holy cross, You have redeemed the world.

Jesus, being stripped of His garments, was violently thrown upon the cross and His hands and feet nailed thereto. In such excruciating pains He remained silent, because it pleased His heavenly Father. He suffered patiently, because He suffered for me. How do I act in sufferings and in troubles? How fretful and impatient, how full of complaints I am!

O Jesus, gracious Lamb of God, I renounce forever my impatience. Crucify, O Lord, my flesh and its concupiscences; scourge, scathe, and punish me in this world, do but spare me in the next. I commit my destiny to You, resigning myself to Your holy will: may it be done in all things!

Our Father who art in heaven, hallowed be Thy name. Thy kingdom come, Thy will be done on earth as it is in heaven. Give us this day our daily bread, and forgive us our debts as we forgive our debtors. Lead us not into temptation but deliver us from evil. Amen.

Hail Mary, full of grace. The Lord is with you. Blessed are you among women, and blessed is the fruit of thy womb. Holy Mary, Mother of God, pray for us sinners now and at the hour of our death. Amen.

Glory be to the Father, and to the Son, and to the Holy Spirit. As it was in the beginning, is now, and ever shall be, world without end. Amen.

Lord Jesus, crucified, have mercy on us!

The Twelfth Station

Jesus is raised upon the Cross and Dies

We adore You, O Christ, and we praise You, because by Your holy cross, You have redeemed the world.

Behold Jesus crucified! Behold His wounds, received for love of you! His whole appearance betokens love: His head is bent to kiss you; His arms are extended to embrace you; His Heart is open to receive you. O superabundance of love, Jesus, the Son of God, dies upon the cross, that man may live and be delivered from everlasting death!

O most amiable Jesus! Who will grant me that I may die for You! I will at least endeavor to die to the world. How must I regard the world and its vanities, when I behold You hanging on the cross, covered with wounds? O Jesus, receive me into Your wounded

Heart: I belong entirely to You; for You alone do I desire to live and to die.

Our Father who art in heaven, hallowed be Thy name. Thy kingdom come, Thy will be done on earth as it is in heaven. Give us this day our daily bread, and forgive us our debts as we forgive our debtors. Lead us not into temptation but deliver us from evil. Amen.

Hail Mary, full of grace. The Lord is with you. Blessed are you among women, and blessed is the fruit of thy womb. Holy Mary, Mother of God, pray for us sinners now and at the hour of our death. Amen.

Glory be to the Father, and to the Son, and to the Holy Spirit. As it was in the beginning, is now, and ever shall be, world without end. Amen.

Lord Jesus, crucified, have mercy on us!

The Thirteenth Station

Jesus is taken from the Cross and given to His Mother

We adore You, O Christ, and we praise You, because by Your holy cross, You have redeemed the world.

Jesus did not descend from the cross but remained on it until He died. And when taken down from it, He in death as in life, rested on the bosom of His divine Mother. Persevere in your resolutions of reform and do not part from the cross; he who perseveres to the end shall be saved. Consider, moreover, how pure the heart should be that receives the body and blood of Christ in the Adorable Sacrament of the Altar.

O Lord Jesus, Your lifeless body, mangled and lacerated, found a worthy resting-place on the bosom of Your virgin Mother. Have I not often compelled You to dwell in my heart, full of sin and impurity as it was? Create in me a new heart, that I may worthily receive Your most sacred body in Holy Communion, and that You may remain in me and I in You for all eternity.

Our Father who art in heaven, hallowed be Thy name. Thy kingdom come, Thy will be done on earth as it is in heaven. Give us this day our daily bread, and forgive us our debts as we forgive our debtors. Lead us not into temptation but deliver us from evil. Amen.

Hail Mary, full of grace. The Lord is with you. Blessed are you among women, and blessed is the fruit of thy womb. Holy Mary, Mother of God, pray for us sinners now and at the hour of our death. Amen.

Glory be to the Father, and to the Son, and to the Holy Spirit. As it was in the beginning, is now, and ever shall be, world without end. Amen.

Lord Jesus, crucified, have mercy on us!

The Fourteenth Station

Jesus is laid in the Sepulcher

We adore You, O Christ, and we praise You, because by Your holy cross, You have redeemed the world.

The body of Jesus is interred in a stranger's sepulchre. He who in this world had not whereupon to rest His head, would not even have a grave of His own, because He was not from this world.

You, who are so attached to the world, henceforth despise it, that you may not perish with it.

O Jesus, You have set me apart from the world; what, then, shall I seek therein? You have created me for Heaven; what, then, have I to do with the world? Depart from me, deceitful world, with Your vanities! Henceforth i will follow the Way of the Cross traced out for me by my Redeemer, and journey onward to my heavenly home, there to dwell forever and ever.

Our Father who art in heaven, hallowed be Thy name. Thy kingdom come, Thy will be done on earth as it is in heaven. Give us this day our daily bread, and forgive us our debts as we forgive our debtors. Lead us not into temptation but deliver us from evil. Amen.

Hail Mary, full of grace. The Lord is with you. Blessed are you among women, and blessed is the fruit of thy womb. Holy Mary, Mother of God, pray for us sinners now and at the hour of our death. Amen.

Glory be to the Father, and to the Son, and to the Holy Spirit. As it was in the beginning, is now, and ever shall be, world without end. Amen.

Lord Jesus, crucified, have mercy on us!

Closing Prayer

Almighty and eternal God, merciful Father, who have given to the human race Your beloved Son as an example of humility, obedience, and patience, to precede us on the way of life, bearing the cross: Graciously grant us that we, inflamed by His infinite love, may take up the sweet yoke of His Gospel together with the mortification of the cross, following Him as His true disciples, so that we shall one day gloriously rise with Him and joyfully hear the final sentence: "Come, ye blessed of My Father, and possess the kingdom which was prepared for you from the beginning," where You reign with the Son and the Holy Ghost, and where we hope to reign with You, world without end. Amen.

Let Creation Praise the Lord

Be praised, my Lord, with all Your creatures,
Especially Brother Sun,

By whom You bring us the day and who brings us the light;
Fair is he and shines with a very great splendor.

Be praised, my Lord, for Sister Moon and the stars,
which you have set clear and lovely in heaven.

Be praised, my Lord, for Brother Wind,
and for air and cloud, calms and all weather.

Be praised, my Lord, for Sister Water,
who is very useful and humble and precious and clean.

Be praised my Lord for Brother Fire, through whom You give us light in
darkness, and he is bright and pleasant and very mighty and strong.

Be praised, my Lord, for our Sister Mother Earth, who sustains us and
keep us, and brings forth fruits and flowers of many colors and leaves.

Praise and bless my Lord, and thank Him,

And serve Him with great humility.

Mediation on Our Father

O Most Holy Our Father: Creator,
Redeemer, Consoler and Our Savior.

Who art in Heaven:
in the Angels and in the Saints;
enlightening them unto knowledge,
because Thou, Lord, art Light,
inflaming them unto love,
because Thou, Lord, art Love;
indwelling and filling them unto blessedness,
because Thou, Lord, art the Highest Good,
the Eternal One,
from whom is every good,
without whom nothing is good.

Hallowed be Thy Name:
may the knowledge of Thee in us be made bright,
so that we may know,
what is the breadth of Thy benefactions,
the length of Thy promises,
the sublimity of Thy Majesty
and the depth of Thy judgments.

Thy Kingdom come:
so that Thou may reign in us by grace
and make us come unto Thy Kingdom,
where vision of Thee is made manifest,
love of Thee made perfect,
company with Thee blessed,
enjoyment of Thee everlasting.

Thy Will be done on Earth as it is in Heaven:
so that we may love Thee with our whole heart
by thinking of Thee always,
with our whole soul by desiring Thee always,
with our whole mind directing unto Thee all our intentions,
by seeking Thy honor in all things
and with all our strength
by expending all our strength
and sense of soul and body in submission to Thy
love and not in anything else;
and may we love our neighbors even as our very selves
by drawing all to Thy love to the extent of our strength,
by rejoicing over the good things of others
just as over our own and by compassionating them in evils
and by giving offense to no one.

Give us this day,
Thy Beloved Son,
Our Lord Jesus Christ,

Our Daily Bread:
to remember and understand and reverence the love,
which He had for us,
and those things,
which He said, did, or endured on our behalf.

And forgive us our debts:
by Thy ineffable Mercy,
and through the virtue of the Passion of Thy Beloved son
and by the merits and intercession of the Blessed Virgin and all
Thy elect.

As we also forgive our debtors:
and what we do not fully forgive,
Lord, make us fully forgive,
so that we may truly love our enemies
for the sake of Thee
and intercede devoutly on their behalf with Thee,

rendering to none evil for evil
and striving in all things to advance unto Thee.

And lead us not into temptation:
hidden or manifest, sudden or importune.

But deliver us from the evil:
past, present, and future.
Glory be to the Father.

Sermon to the Birds

My little sisters, the birds, much bounden are ye unto God, your Creator, and always in every place ought ye to praise Him, for that He hath given you liberty to fly about everywhere, and hath also given you double and triple rainment; moreover He preserved your seed in the ark of Noah, that your race might not perish out of the world; still more are ye beholden to Him for the element of the air which He hath appointed for you; beyond all this, ye sow not, neither do you reap; and God feedeth you, and giveth you the streams and fountains for your drink; the mountains and valleys for your refuge and the high trees whereon to make your nests; and because ye know not how to spin or sow, God clotheth you, you and your children; wherefore your Creator loveth you much, seeing that He hath bestowed on you so many benefits; and therefore, my little sisters, beware of the sin of ingratitude, and study always to give praises unto God.

Made in the USA
Las Vegas, NV
21 January 2021